Arthur Symons, Mathilde Blind

A Selection From the Poems of Mathilde Blind

Arthur Symons, Mathilde Blind

A Selection From the Poems of Mathilde Blind

ISBN/EAN: 9783744713214

Printed in Europe, USA, Canada, Australia, Japan

Cover: Foto ©Thomas Meinert / pixelio.de

More available books at **www.hansebooks.com**

A Selection

FROM THE

Poems

OF

Mathilde Blind

EDITED BY
ARTHUR SYMONS

London
T. FISHER UNWIN
PATERNOSTER SQUARE
1897

INTRODUCTION.

TO Mathilde Blind all life was an emotion; and thought, to her, was of the same substance as feeling. That is why she has been able, in verse, to express a vivid personality, in what may often seem to be an impersonal way. *The Ascent of Man*, her largest work, is a hymn of religious ecstasy; for the scientific teaching of Darwin, to most people a very negative sort of gospel, inflamed her with the ardour of a worshipper: she believed it, by an act of faith, as the devout Christian believes in the mysteries of his church. And in all her expressions of strenuous and reverent unbelief, which rise at times to almost the very highest rapture of Pantheism, she is giving voice to what was really deepest in her nature: a sort of universal passion, which found its keenest satisfaction in the giving up of " puny personal joy and pain," its finest reward in a perhaps vague, yet closely realised, and certainly " deathless " hope.

This instinct for what was religious, and thus emotional, in all thought, helped her to write, with an eloquence which was essentially sympathy, about many lands, and the landscapes of many religions; and finally, about the gods and sands of Egypt; for Egypt, more than any other country, seems to perpetuate, in somewhat desolate a splendour, the eternal elements of humanity. It was through the same instinct that she came to write her poems of what seemed to her rather a realistic kind: *The Heather on Fire*, and some of the *Dramas in Miniature*. She apprehended human life as something pitiful, to be succoured; never as something interesting, to be observed. It was the enthusiasm of an idea or an ideal which absorbed her in certain problems of sin, injustice, misery: a universal human pity, of which, in some curious way, as of self-pity, her very personal poems have their share. Of this human sympathy, as of that religious sentiment, art was never, to her, more than the servant.

She was a poet, almost in spite of herself. It was direct, and not directed, emotion which gave her verse its share of that rapture without which poetry cannot exist. But she had confidence in the plenary inspiration of first thoughts; and her work remains a suggestion, rather than an accomplishment, of what she might have done. Such as it is, and such as I have tried to represent it, at its best, in this selection, it is a memorial more intimately human, more immediately the utterance of a particular, most brave and ardent soul, than almost any similar body of poetic work. To those who knew her, it is like the sound of her voice; and I think it must have, to those who know her only by her books, the accent of a voice that seems, the first time it is heard, to be remembered.

ARTHUR SYMONS.

ROME, *Feb.* 13, 1897.

CONTENTS.

POEMS OF THE EAST AND WEST:—   PAGE

The Mystic's Vision 1
The Pilgrim Soul 4
The Tombs of the Kings 16
The Moon of Ramadân 24
The Dying Dragoman 28
The Teamster 34
Noonday Rest 42
The Street-Children's Dance 44

POEMS OF THE OPEN AIR:—

The Sower 49
Reapers 51
The Sleeping Beauty 52
Apple-Blossom 53
A Winter Landscape 55
In the St. Gotthardt Pass 56
Roman Anemones 57
On Reading the "Rubáiyát" of Omar Khayyám 58
The Moat 59
On a Torso of Cupid 60
The Mirror of Diana 62

CONTENTS.

PAGE

LOVE IN EXILE AND OTHER LOVE POEMS:—

Love in Exile 65
L'Envoi 99
The Songs of Summer 103
On and On 104
Cross-Roads 106
The Forest Pool 107
Once We Played 108
Only a Smile 109
Sometimes I Wonder 110
Many Will Love You 111
Affinities 112

SONGS AND SONNETS:—

Song 115
Pastiche 116
A Fantasy 117
On a Viola d'Amore 120
Soul-Drift 122
Lassitude 123
Rest 124

SONNETS:—

Sleep 125
Dead Love 126
Despair 127
Cleave Thou the Waves 128

SONNETS (*continued*).

	PAGE
The Dead	129
Hope	130
Time's Shadow	131
Suffering	132
Ἀνάγκη	133
To Memory	134
The After-Glow	135
Manchester by Night	136
The Red Sunsets, 1883	137
The Sâkiyeh	138
Mourning Women	139
The Agnostic	140
Heart's-Ease	141
Untimely Love	142
Christmas Eve	143
The Evening of the Year	144
New Year's Eve	145
Nirvana	146

Poems of the East and West.

THE MYSTIC'S VISION.

AH! I shall kill myself with dreams!
   These dreams that softly lap me round
Through trance-like hours, in which, meseems,
   That I am swallowed up and drowned;
Drowned in your love which flows o'er me
As o'er the seaweed flows the sea.

In watches of the middle night,
   'Twixt vesper and 'twixt matin bell,
With rigid arms and straining sight,
   I wait within my narrow cell;
With muttered prayers, suspended will,
I wait your advent—statue-still.

Across the Convent garden walls
   The wind blows from the silver seas;
Black shadow of the cypress falls
   Between the moon-meshed olive trees;
Sleep-walking from their golden bowers,
Flit disembodied orange flowers.

And in God's consecrated house,
    All motionless from head to feet,
My heart awaits her heavenly Spouse,
    As white I lie on my white sheet;
With body lulled and soul awake,
I watch in anguish for your sake.

And suddenly, across the gloom,
    The naked moonlight sharply swings;
A Presence stirs within the room,
    A breath of flowers and hovering wings:
Your Presence without form and void,
Beyond all earthly joys enjoyed.

My heart is hushed, my tongue is mute,
    My life is centred in your will;
You play upon me like a lute
    Which answers to its master's skill,
Till passionately vibrating,
Each nerve becomes a throbbing string.

Oh, incommunicably sweet!
    No longer aching and apart,
As rain upon the tender wheat,
    You pour upon my thirsty heart;
As scent is bound up in the rose,
Your love within my bosom glows.

Unseen, untouched, unheard, unknown,
   You take possession of your bride ;
I lose myself to live alone
   In you, who once were crucified
For me, that now would die in you,
As in the sun a drop of dew.

Fish may not perish in the deep,
   Nor sparrows fall through yielding air,
Pure gold in hottest flame will keep ;
   How should I fail and falter where
You are, O Lord, in whose control
For ever lies my living soul?

Ay, break through every wall of sense,
   And pierce my flesh as nails did pierce
Your bleeding limbs in anguish tense,
   And torture me with bliss so fierce,
That self dies out, as die it must,
Ashes to ashes, dust to dust.

Thus let me die, so loved and lost,
   Annihilated in my dreams !
Nor force me, an unwilling ghost,
   To face the loud day's brutal beams ;
The noisy world's inanities,
All vanity of vanities.

THE PILGRIM SOUL.

THROUGH the winding mazes of windy streets
   Blindly I hurried I knew not wither,
Through the dim-lit ways of the brain thus fleets

A fluttering dream driven hither and thither.—
The fitful flare of the moon fled fast,
Like a sickly smile now seeming to wither,

Now dark like a scowl in the hurrying blast
As ominous shadows swept over the roofs
Where white as a ghost the scared moonlight had passed.

Curses came mingled with wails and reproofs,
With doors banging to and the crashing of glass,
With the baying of dogs and the clatter of hoofs,

With the rush of the river as, huddling its mass
Of weltering water towards the deep ocean,
'Neath many-arched bridges its eddies did pass.

A hubbub of voices in savage commotion
Was mixed with the storm in a chaos of sound,
And thrilled as with ague in shuddering emotion

I fled as the hunted hare flees from the hound.
Past churches whose bells were tumultuously ringing
The year in, and clashing in concord around ;

Past the deaf walls of dungeons whose curses seemed
   clinging
To the tempest that shivered and shrieked in amaze-
   ment ;
Past brightly lit mansions whence music and singing

Came borne like a scent through the close-curtained
   casement,
To vaults in whose shadow wild outcasts were hiding
Their misery deep in the gloom of the basement ;

By vociferous taverns where women were biding
With features all withered, distorted, aghast ;
Some sullenly silent, some brutally chiding,

Some reeling away into gloom as I passed
On, on, through lamp-lighted and fountain-filled
   places,
Where throned in rich temples, resplendent and vast,

The Lord of the City is deafened with praises
As worshipping multitudes kneel as of old ;
Nor care for the crowds of cadaverous faces,

The men that are marred and the maids that are sold—
Inarticulate masses promiscuously jumbled
And crushed 'neath their Juggernaut idol of gold.

Lost lives of great cities bespattered and tumbled,
Black rags the rain soaks, the wind whips like a knout,
Were crouched in the streets there, and o'er them nigh stumbled

A swarm of light maids as they tripped to some rout.
The silk of their raiment voluptuously hisses
And flaps o'er the flags as loud laughing they flout

The wine-maddened men they ne'er satiate with kisses
For the pearls and the diamonds that make them more fair,
For the flash of large jewels that fire them with blisses,

For the glitter of gold in the gold of their hair.
They smiled and they cozened, their bold eyes shone brightly
And lightened with laughter, as, lit by the flare

Of the wind-fretted gas-lamps, they footed it lightly,
Or, closely enlacing and bowered in gloom,
With mouth pressed to hot mouth, their parched lips
    drain nightly

The wine-cup of pleasure red-sealing their doom ;
Brief lives like bright rockets which, aridly glowing,
Fall burnt out to ashes and reel to the tomb.

On, on, loud and louder the rough night was blowing,
Shrill singing was mixed with strange cries of
    despair ;
And high overhead the black sky, redly glowing,

Loomed over the city one ominous glare,
As dark yawning funnels from foul throats for ever
Belched smoke grimly flaming, which outraged the
    air.

On, on, by long quays where the lamps in the river
Were writhing like serpents that hiss ere they drown,
And poplars with palsy seemed coldly to shiver,

On, on, to the bare desert end of the town.
When lo ! the wind stopped like a heart that's ceased
    beating,
And naught but the waters, white foaming and brown,

Were heard as to seaward their currents went fleeting.
But hark ! o'er the lull breaks a desolate moan,
Like a little lost lamb's that is timidly bleating

When, strayed from the shepherd, it staggers alone
By tracks which the mountain stream shake with
    their thunder,
Where death seems to gape from each boulder and
    stone.

I turned to the murmur : the clouds swept asunder
And wheeled like white sea-gulls around the white
    moon ;
And the moon, like a white maid, looked down in
    mute wonder

On a boy whose wan eyelids were closed as in swoon.
Half nude on the ground he lay, wasted and chilly,
And torn as with thorns and sharp brambles of June ;

His hair, like a flame which at twilight burns stilly,
In a halo of light round his temples was blown,
And his tears fell like rain on a storm-stricken lily

Where he lay on the cold ground, abandoned, alone.
With heart moved towards him in wondering pity,
I tenderly seized his thin hand with my own :

Crying, "Child, say how cam'st thou so far from the
    city?
How cam'st thou alone in such pitiful plight,
All blood-stained thy feet, with rags squalid and
    gritty,

A waif by the wayside, unhoused in the night?"
Then rose he and lifted the bright locks, storm driven,
Which flamed round his forehead and clouded his
    sight,

And mournful as meres on a moorland at even
His blue eyes flashed wildly through tears as they
    fell ;
Strange eyes full of horror, yet fuller of heaven,

Like eyes that from heaven have looked upon hell,
The eyes of an angel whose depths show where,
    burning
And lost in the pit, toss the angels that fell.

" Ah," wailed he in tones full of agonized yearning,
Like the plaintive lament of a sickening dove
On a surf-beaten shore, when it sees past returning

The wings of the wild flock fast fading above,
As they melt on the sky-line like foam-flakes in
    motion :
So sadly he wailed, " I am Love ! I am Love !

"Behold me cast out as weed spurned of the ocean,
Half nude on the bare ground, and covered with
   scars
I perish of cold here;" and, choked with emotion,

Gave a sob: at the low sob a shower of stars
Broke shuddering from heaven, pale flaming, and fell
Where the mid-city roared as with rumours of wars.

"Be these God's tears?" I cried, as my tears 'gan to
   well.
"Ah, Love, I have sought thee in temples and
   towers,
In shrines where men pray, and in marts where they
   sell;

"In tapestried chambers made tropic with flowers,
Where amber-haired women, soft breathing of spice,
Lay languidly lapped in the gold-dropping showers

Which gladdened and maddened their amorous eyes.
I have looked for thee vainly in churches where
   beaming
The Saints glowed embalmed in a prism of dyes,

" Where wave over wave the rapt music went streaming
With breakers of sound in full anthems elate.
I have asked, but none knew thee, or knew but thy seeming ;

" A mask in thy likeness on high seats of state ;
And they bound it with gold, and they crowned it with glory,
This thing they called love, which was bond slave to hate.

" And they bowed down before it with brown heads and hoary,
They worshipped it nightly, loud hymning its praise,
While out in the cold blast, none heeding its story,

" Love staggers, an outcast, with lust in its place."
Love shivered and sighed like a reed that is shaken,
And lifting his hunger-nipped face to my face :

" Nay, if of the world I must needs die forsaken,
Say thou wilt not leave me to dearth and despair.
To thy heart, to thy home, let the exile be taken,

"And feed me and shelter——" "Where, outcast,
   ah, where?
Like thee I am homeless and spurned of all mortals;
The House of my fathers yawns wide to the air.

" Stalks desolation across the void portals,
Hope lies aghast on the ruinous floor,
The halls that were thronged once with star-browed
   immortals,

" With gods statue-still o'er the world-whirr and roar,
With fauns of the forest and nymphs of the river,
Are cleft as if lightning had struck to their core.

" The luminous ceilings, where soaring for ever
Dim hosts of plumed angels smoked up to the sky,
With God-litten faces that yearned to the giver

" As vapours of morning the sun draws on high,
Now ravaged with rain hear the hollow winds whistle
Through rifts in the rafters which echo their cry.

" Blest walls that were vowed to the Virgin now
   bristle
With weeds of sick scarlet and plague-spotted moss,
And stained on the ground, choked with thorn and
   rank thistle,

"Rots a worm-eaten Christ on a mouldering Cross.
From the House of my fathers, distraught, broken-hearted,
With a pang of immense, irredeemable loss,

"On my wearying pilgrimage blindly I started
To seek thee, oh Love, in high places and low,
And instead of the glories for ever departed,

"To warm my starved life in thy mightier glow.
For I deemed thee a Presence ringed round with all splendour,
With a sceptre in hand and a crown on thy brow;

"And, behold, thou art helpless—most helpless to tender
Thy service to others, who needest their care.
Yea, now that I find thee a weak child and slender,

"Exposed to the blast of the merciless air,
Like a lamb that is shorn, like a leaf that is shaken,
What, Love, now is left but to die in despair?

"For Death is the mother of all the forsaken,
The grave a strait bed where she rocks them to rest,
And sleep, from whose silence they never shall waken,

"The balm of oblivion she sheds on their breast."
Then I seized him and led to the brink of the river,
Where two storm-beaten seagulls were fluttering west,

And the lamplight in drowning seemed coldly to shiver,
And clasping Love close for the leap from on high,
Said—"Let us go hence, Love; go home, Love, for ever;

"For life casts us forth, and Man dooms us to die."
As if stung by a snake the Child shuddered and started,
And clung to me close with a passionate cry:

"Stay with me, stay with me, poor, broken-hearted;
Pain, if not pleasure, we two will divide;
Though with the sins of the world I have smarted,

"Though with the shame of the world thou art dyed,
Weak as I am, on thy breast I'll recover,
Worn as thou art, thou shalt bloom as my bride:

"Bloom as the flower of the World for the lover
Whom thou hast found in a lost little Child."
And as he kissed my lips over and over—

Child now, or Man, was it who thus beguiled ?—
Even as I looked on him, Love waxing slowly,
Grew as a little cloud, floating enisled,

Which spreads out aloft in the blue sky till solely
It fills the deep ether tremendous in height,
With far-flashing snow-peaks and pinnacles wholly

Invisible, vanishing light within light.
So changing waxed Love—till he towered before me,
Outgrowing my lost gods in stature and might.

As he grew, as he drew me, a great awe came o'er me,
And stammering, I shook as I questioned his name;
But gently bowed o'er me, he soothèd and bore me,

Yea, bore once again to the haunts whence I came,
By dark ways and dreary, by rough roads and gritty,
To the penfolds of sin, to the purlieus of shame.

And lo, as we went through the woe-clouded city,
Where women bring forth and men labour in vain,
Weak Love grew so great in his passion of pity
That all who beheld him were born once again.

THE TOMBS OF THE KINGS.

WHERE the mummied Kings of Egypt, wrapped in linen fold on fold,
Couched for ages in their coffins, crowned with crowns of dusky gold,

Lie in subterranean chambers, biding to the day of doom,
Counterfeit life's hollow semblance in each mazy mountain tomb,

Grisly in their gilded coffins, mocking masks of skin and bone,
Yet remain in change unchanging, balking Nature of her own;

Mured in mighty Mausoleums, walled in from the night and day,
Lo, the mortal Kings of Egypt hold immortal Death at bay.

For—so spake the Kings of Egypt—those colossal ones whose hand
Held the peoples from Pitasa to the Kheta's conquered land;

Who, with flash and clash of lances and war-chariots, stormed and won
Many a town of stiff-necked Syria to high-towering Askalon:

"We have been the faithful stewards of the deathless gods on high;
We have built them starry temples underneath the starry sky.

"We have smitten rebel nations, as a child is whipped with rods:
We the living incarnation of imperishable gods.

"Shall we suffer Death to trample us to nothingness? and must
We be scattered, as the whirlwind blows about the desert dust?

"No! Death shall not dare come near us, nor Corruption shall not lay
Hands upon our sacred bodies, incorruptible as day.

"Let us put a bit and bridle, and rein in Time's headlong course;
Let us ride him through the ages as a master rides his horse.

"On the changing earth unchanging let us bide till Time shall end,
Till, reborn in blest Osiris, mortal with Immortal blend."

Yea, so spake the Kings of Egypt, they whose lightest word was law,
At whose nod the far-off nations cowered, stricken dumb with awe.

And Fate left the haughty rulers to work out their monstrous doom;
And, embalmed with myrrh and ointments, they were carried to the tomb;

Through the gate of Bab-el-Molouk, where the sulphur hills lie bare,
Where no green thing casts a shadow in the noon's tremendous glare;

Where the unveiled Blue of heaven in its bare intensity
Weighs upon the awestruck spirit with the world's immensity;

Through the Vale of Desolation, where no beast or bird draws breath,
To the Coffin-Hills of Tuat—the Metropolis of Death.

Down—down—down into the darkness, where, on
either hand, dread Fate,
In the semblance of a serpent, watches by the dolorous
gate ;

Down—down—down into the darkness, where no
gleam of sun or star
Sheds its purifying radiance from the living world
afar ;

Where in labyrinthine windings, darkly hidden, down
and down,—
Proudly on his marble pillow, with old Egypt's double
crown,

And his mien of cold commandment, grasping still his
staff of state,
Rests the mightiest of the Pharaohs, whom the world
surnamed the Great.

Swathed in fine Sidonian linen, crossed hands folded
on the breast,
There the mummied Kings of Egypt lie within each
painted chest.

And upon their dusky foreheads Pleiades of flaming
   gems,
Glowing through the nether darkness, flash from
   luminous diadems.

Where is Memphis? Like a Mirage, melted into
   empty air :
But these royal gems yet sparkle richly on their raven
   hair.

Where is Thebes in all her glory, with her gates of
   beaten gold ?
Where Syenê, or that marvel, Heliopolis of old ?

Where is Edfu? Where Abydos? Where those
   pillared towns of yore
Whose auroral temples glittered by the Nile's thick-
   peopled shore ?

Gone as evanescent cloudlands, Alplike in the after-
   glow ;
But these Kings hold fast their bodies of four thousand
   years ago.

Sealed up in their Mausoleums, in the bowels of the
   hills,
There they hide from dissolution and Death's swiftly
   grinding mills.

Scattering fire, Uræus serpents guard the Tombs'
    tremendous gate ;
While Thoth holds the trembling balance, weighs the
    heart and seals its fate.

And a multitude of mummies in the swaddling clothes
    of death,
Ferried o'er the sullen river, on and on still hasteneth.

And around them and above them, blazoned on the
    rocky walls,
Crowned with stars, enlaced by serpents, in divine
    processionals,

Ibis-headed, jackal-featured, vulture-hooded, pass on
    high,
Gods on gods through Time's perspectives—pilgrims
    of Eternity.

There, revealed by fitful flashes, in a gloom that may
    be felt,
Wild Chimæras flash from darkness, glittering like
    Orion's belt.

And on high, o'er shining waters, in their barks the
    gods sail by,
In the Sunboat and the Moonboat, rowed across the
    rose-hued sky.

Night, that was before Creation, watches sphinx-like,
   starred with eyes,
And the hours and days are passing, and the years and
   centuries.

But these mummied Kings of Egypt, pictures of a
   perished race,
Lie, of busy Death forgotten, face by immemorial
   face.

Though the glorious sun above them, burning on the
   naked plain,
Clothes the empty wildernesses with the golden, glow-
   ing grain ;

Though the balmy Moon above them, floating in the
   milky Blue,
Fills the empty wildernesses with a silver fall of dew ;

Though life comes and flies unresting, like the shadow
   which a dove
Casts upon the Sphinx, in passing, for a moment from
   above ;—

Still these mummied Kings of Egypt, wrapped in
   linen, fold on fold,
Bide through ages in their coffins, crowned with
   crowns of dusky gold.

Had the sun once brushed them lightly, or a breath
  of air, they must
Instantaneously have crumbled into evanescent dust.

Pale and passive in their prisons, they have conquered
  chained to death;
And their lineaments look living now as when they
  last drew breath!

Have they conquered? Oh the pity of those Kings
  within their tombs,
Locked in stony isolation in those petrifying glooms!

Motionless where all is motion in a rolling Universe,
Heaven, by answering their prayer, turned it to a
  deadly curse;

Left them fixed where all is fluid in a world of star-
  winged skies;
Where, in myriad transformations, all things pass and
  nothing dies;

Nothing dies but what is tethered, kept when Time
  would set it free,
To fulfil Thought's yearning tension upward through
  Eternity.

THE MOON OF RAMADÂN.

THE sunset melts upon the Nile,
　　The stony desert glows,
Beneath heaven's universal smile,
　　One burning damask rose;
And like a Peri's pearly boat,
　　No longer than a span,
Look, faint on fiery sky afloat,
　　The Moon of Ramadân.

Our boat drifts idly with the Stream,
　　Our boatmen ship the oar;
Vistas of endless temples gleam
　　On either topaz shore;
And swimming over groves of Palm,
　　A crescent weak and wan,
There steals into the perfect calm
　　The Moon of Ramadân.

THE MOON OF RAMADÂN.

All nature seems to bask in peace
 And hush her lowest sigh ;
Above the river's golden fleece
 The happy Halcyons fly.
And lost in some old lotos dream,
 The pensive Pelican
Sees mirrored in the mazy stream
 The Moon of Ramadân.

Black outlined on the golden air,
 A turbaned Silhouette,
The Mueddin invites to prayer
 From many a Minaret.
Our dusky boatmen hear the call,
 And prostrate, man on man,
They bow, adoring, one and all,
 The Moon of Ramadân.

Where Luxor's rose-flushed columns shine
 Above the river's brim,
The priest with incense once, and wine,
 Made sacrifice to Him,
The highest god of Thebes, and head
 Of all the heavenly clan ;
But now the Moslem hails instead
 The Moon of Ramadân.

The gods have come, the gods have gone,
    Yet wedded to their walls,
Winged with the serpent of the Sun
    In mute processionals,
They stride from door to massy door,
    Bound nations in their van,
Though Amon's Sun has waned before
    The Moon of Ramadân.

Yea, even proud Egypt's proudest king,
    Who chastised rebel lands,
And brought his gods for offering
    Mountains of severed hands ;
Who singly, like a god of War,
    Smote hosts that swerved and ran,
Lies low 'neath Allah's scimetar—
    The Moon of Ramadân.

And Isis, Queen, whose sacred disk's
    Horned splendour crowned her brow,
While fires of flashing Obelisks
    Flamed in the Afterglow ;
And white-robed priests who served her shrine
    Have turned Mahommedan,
And worship Him who wears for sign
    The Moon of Ramadân.

THE MOON OF RAMADÂN.

The rosy lotos, flower and leaf,
   Which wreathed each sacred lake,
With Nature's loveliest bas-relief,
   Has followed in their wake;
Yea, with the last true Pharaoh's death,
   The lotos leaves, grown wan,
Have changed to lily white beneath
   The Moon of Ramadân.

The gods may come, the gods may go,
   And royal realms change hands;
But the most ancient Nile will flow,
   And flood the desert sands;
And nightly will he glass the stars'
   Unearthly caravan,
Nor care if it be Rome's red Mars
   Or Moon of Ramadân.

The sunset fades upon the Nile;
   The desert's stony gloom,
Receding blankly mile on mile,
   Grows silent as a tomb.
All weary wanderers, man and beast,
   Hie, fasting, to the Khan,
While shines above their nightly feast
   The Moon of Ramadân.

THE DYING DRAGOMAN.

FAR in the fiery wilderness,
    Beyond the town of Assouan,
Left languishing in sore distress,
    There lay a dying Dragoman.
Alone amid the waste, alone,
The hot sand burnt him to the bone;
And on his breast, like heated stone,
    The burden of the air did press.

His head was pillowed on a tomb,
    Reared to some holy Sheik of old;
The irresistible Simoom
    Whirled drifts of sand that rose and rolled
Around him, and the panting air
Was one sulphureous spectral glare,
Shot with such gleams as lights the lair
    Of tigers in a jungle's gloom.

Groaning, he closed his bloodshot eyes,
   As if to shut out all he feared;
And greedily a swarm of flies
   Fell on his face and tangled beard.
He lay like one who ne'er would lift
His head above that ashy drift;
When lo, there gleamed across a rift
   The blue oasis of the skies.

Like smoke dispersing far and wide,
   The draggled sands were blown away;
The wild clouds in a refluent tide
   Receded from the face of day.
The lingering airs yet lightly blew
Till the last speck cleared out of view,
And left the hushed Eternal Blue,
   And nothing else beside.

Then once again, with change of moods,
   A mighty shadow, broadening, fell
Across those shadeless solitudes,
   Without a Palm, without a Well.
Wing wedged in wing, an ordered mass
Unnumbered numbers pass and pass,
As if one Will, one only, was
   In all those moving multitudes.

A chord thrilled in the sick man's brain;
  He raised his heavy-lidded eyes,
He raised his heavy head with pain,
  And caught a glimpse of netted skies,
Meshed in ten thousand wings in flight
That cleft the air. Oh wondrous sight!
He gasped, he shrieked in sheer delight:
  "The Storks! The Storks fly home again!

"I too, O Storks, I too, even I,
  Would see my native land again.
Oh, had I wings that I might fly
  With you, wild birds, across the main!
Take, take me to the land, I pray,
The land where nests are full in May,
The land where my young children play:
  Oh, take me with you, or I die.

"My lonely heart blooms like a flower,
  My children, when I think of you;
My love is like an April shower,
  And fills my heart with drops of dew.
Along their unknown tracks, ah me!
The Storks will fly across the sea;
My children soon will hail with glee
  Their red bills on the rain-washed tower."

Home-sickness seized him for the herds
   That browse upon the fresh green leas ;
Home-sickness for the cuckoo birds
   That shout afar in feathery trees ;
For running stream and rippling rill
That, racing, turned his woodland mill :
And tears on tears began to fill
   His eyes, confusing all he sees.

Again he doats on rosy cheeks
   Of children rolling in the grass ;
Again the busy days and weeks,
   The months and years serenely pass.
Black forest clocks tick day and night,
His board and bed are snowy white,
His humble house is just as bright
   As if it were a house of glass.

Again, beneath the high-peaked roof,
   His wife's unresting shuttle flies
Across the even warp and woof ;
   Again his thrifty mother plies
Her wheel, that hums like noontide bees ;
And lint-locked babes about her knees
Hark to strange tales of talking trees,
   And Storks deep versed in sage replies.

Again the ring of swinging chimes
   Calls all the pious folk to church,
With shining Sunday face, betimes,
   Through rustling woods of beech and birch
Full of moist glimmering hollows where
The pines bow murmuring as in prayer,
And musically through the air
   The forest's mighty Choral swells.

Again, O Lord, again he sees
   The place where Heaven came down one day;
Where, in a space of bloom and bees,
   He won his wife one morn of May.
Warm pulses shook and thrilled his blood,
Wild birds were singing in the wood,
The flowering world in bridal mood
   Joined in the Pinewood's symphonies.

Again, O Lord, in grief and fear,
   He bids good-bye to all he loves;
The waters swell, the woods are sere,
   The Storks are gone, and hushed the doves.
He goes with them; he goes to heal
The sickness whose insidious seal
Is set on him. Ah, tears will steal
   And blur the Storks that disappear.

A furnace fire behind the hill,
   The sun has burnt itself away ;
The ghost of light, transparent, chill,
   Yet floats upon the edge of day.
And all the desert holds its breath
As if it felt and crouched beneath
The filmy, flying bat of death
   About a heart for ever still.

And one by one, seraphic, bland,
   The bright stars open in the skies ;
And large above the Shadow land
   The white-faced moon begins to rise.
And all the wilderness grows wan
Beneath the stars, that one by one
Look down upon the lifeless man
   As if they were his children's eyes.

THE TEAMSTER.

WITH slow and slouching gait Sam leads the team;
   He stoops i' the shoulders, worn with work not years;
One only passion has he, it would seem—
   The passion for the horses which he rears:
He names them as one would some household pet,
       May, Violet.

He thinks them quite as sensible as men;
   As nice as women, but not near so skittish;
He fondles, cossets, scolds them now and then,
   Nay, gravely talks as if they knew good British:
You hear him call from dawn to set of sun,
       "Goo back! Com on!"

Sam never seems depressed nor yet elate,
   Like Nature's self he goes his punctual round;
On Sundays, smoking by his garden gate,
   For hours he'll stand, with eyes upon the ground,
Like some tired cart-horse in a field alone,
       And still as stone.

Yet, howsoever stolid he may seem,
  Sam has his tragic background, weird and wild
Like some adventure in a drunkard's dream.
  Impossible, you'd swear, for one so mild :
Yet village gossips dawdling o'er their ale
    Still tell the tale.

In his young days Sam loved a servant-maid,
  A girl with happy eyes like hazel brooks
That dance i' the sun, cheeks as if newly made
  Of pouting roses coyly hid in nooks,
And warm brown hair that wantoned into curl :
    A fresh-blown girl.

Sam came a-courting while the year was blithe,
  When wet browed mowers, stepping out in tune,
With level stroke and rhythmic swing of scythe,
  Smote down the proud grass in the pomp of June,
And waggons, half-tipped over, seemed to sway
    With loads of hay.

The elder bush beside the orchard croft
  Brimmed over with its bloom like curds and cream ;
From out grey nests high in the granary loft
  Black clusters of small heads with callow scream
Peered open-beaked, as swallows flashed along
    To feed their young.

Ripening towards the harvest swelled the wheat,
    Lush cherries dangled 'gainst the latticed panes;
The roads were baking in the windless heat,
    And dust had floured the glossy country lanes,
One sun-hushed, light-flushed Sunday afternoon,
        The last of June,

When, with his thumping heart all out of joint,
    And pulses beating like a stroller's drum,
Sam screwed his courage to the sticking point
    And asked his blushing sweetheart if she'd come
To Titsey Fair; he meant to coax coy May
        To name the day.

But her rich master snapped his thumb and swore
    The girl was not for him! Should not go out!
And, whistling to his dogs, slammed-to the door
    Close in Sam's face, and left him dazed without
In the fierce sunshine, blazing in his path .
        Like fire of wrath.

Unheeding, he went forth with hot wild eyes
    Past fields of feathery oats and wine-red clover;
Unheeded, larks soared singing to the skies,
    Or rang the plaintive cry of rising plover;
Unheeded, pheasants with a startled sound
        Whirred from the ground.

On, on he went by acres full of grain,
  By trees and meadows reeling past his sight,
As to a man whirled onward in a train
  The land with spinning hedgerows seems in flight;
At last he stopped and leant a long, long while
    Against a stile.

Hours passed; the clock struck ten; a hush of night,
  In which even wind and water seemed at peace;
But here and there a glimmering cottage light
  Shone like a glowworm through the slumberous trees;
Or from some far-off homestead through the dark
    A watch-dog's bark.

But all at once Sam gave a stifled cry:
  "There's fire," he muttered, "fire upon the hills!"
No fire—but as the late moon rose on high
  Her light looked smoke-red as through belching mills:
No fire—but moonlight turning in his path
    To fire of wrath.

He looked abroad with eyes that gave the mist
  A lurid tinge above the breadths of grain
Owned by May's master. Then he shook his fist,
  Still muttering, "Fire!" and measured o'er again
The road he'd come, where, lapped in moonlight, lay
    Huge ricks of hay.

There he paused glaring. Then he turned and waned
  Like mist into the misty, moon-soaked night,
Where the pale silvery fields were blotched and stained
  With strange fantastic shadows. But what light
Is that which leaps up, flickering lithe and long,
    With licking tongue !

Hungry it darts and hisses, twists and turns,
  And with each minute shoots up high and higher,
Till, wrapped in flames, the mighty hayrick burns
  And sends its sparks on to a neighbouring byre,
Where, frightened at the hot, tremendous glow,
    The cattle low.

And rick on rick takes fire ; and next a stye,
  Whence through the smoke the little pigs rush out ;
The house-dog barks ; then, with a startled cry,
  The window is flung open, shout on shout
Wakes the hard-sleeping farm where man and maid
    Start up dismayed.

And with wild faces wavering in the glare,
  In nightcaps, bedgowns, clothes half huddled on,
Some to the pump, some to the duck-pond tear
  In frantic haste, while others splashing run
With pails, or turn the hose with flame-scorched face
    Upon the blaze.

At last, when some wan streaks began to show
   In the chill darkness of the sky, the fire
Went out, subdued but for the sputtering glow
   Of sparks among wet ashes. Barn and byre
Were safe, but swallowed all the summer math
       By fire of wrath.

Still haggard from the night's wild work and pale,
   Farm-men and women stood in whispering knots,
Regaled with foaming mugs of nut-brown ale;
   Firing his oaths about like vicious shots,
The farmer hissed out now and then: "Gad damn!
       It's that black Sam."

They had him up and taxed him with the crime;
   Denying naught, he sulked and held his peace;
And so, a branded convict, in due time,
   Handcuffed and cropped, they shipped him overseas:
Seven years of shame sliced from his labourer's life
       As with a knife.

But through it all the image of a girl
   With hazel eyes like pebbled waters clear,
And warm brown hair that wantoned into curl,
   Kept his heart sweet through many a galling year,
Like to a bit of lavender long pressed
       In some black chest.

At last his time was up, and Sam returned
  To his dear village with its single street,
Where, in the sooty forge, the fire still burned,
  As, hammering on the anvil, red with heat,
The smith wrought at a shoe with tongues aglow,
    Blow upon blow.

There stood the church, with peals for death and birth,
  Its ancient spire o'ertopping ancient trees,
And there the graves and mounds of unknown earth,
  Gathered like little children round its knees;
There was " The Bull," with sign above the door,
    And sanded floor.

Unrecognised Sam took his glass of beer,
  And picked up gossip which the men let fall:
How Farmer Clow had failed, and one named Steer
  Had taken on the land, repairs and all;
And how the Kimber girl was to be wed
    To Betsy's Ned.

Sam heard no more, flung down his pence, and took
  The way down to the well-remembered stile;
There, in the gloaming by the trysting brook,
  He came upon his May—with just that smile
For sheep-faced Ned, that light in happy eyes:
    Oh, sugared lies!

He came upon them with black-knitted brows
  And clenched brown hands, and muttered huskily:
"Oh, little May, are those your true love's vows
  You swore to keep while I was over-sea?"
Then crying, turned upon the other one,
        "Com on, com on."

Then they fell to with faces set for fight,
  And hit each other hard with rustic pride;
But Sam, whose arm with iron force could smite,
  Knocked his cowed rival down, and won his bride.
May wept and smiled, swayed like a wild red rose
        As the wind blows.

She married Sam, who loved her with a wild
  Strong love he could not put to words—too deep
For her to gauge; but with her first-born child
  May dropped off, flower-like, into the long sleep,
And left him nothing but the memory of
        His little love.

Since then the silent teamster lives alone,
  The trusted headman of his master Steer;
One only passion seems he still to own—
  The passion for the foals he has to rear;
And still the prettiest, full of life and play,
        Is little May.

NOONDAY REST.

THE willows whisper very, very low
    Unto the listening breeze ;
Sometimes they lose a leaf which, flickering slow,
    Faints on the sunburnt leas.

Beneath the whispering boughs and simmering skies,
    On the hot ground at rest,
Still as a stone, a ragged woman lies,
    Her baby at the breast.

Nibbling around her browse monotonous sheep,
    Flies buzz about her head ;
Her heavy eyes are shuttered by a sleep
    As of the slumbering dead.

The happy birds that live to love and sing,
    Flitting from bough to bough,
Peer softly at this ghastly human thing
    With grizzled hair and brow.

O'er what strange ways may not these feet have trod
   That match the cracking clay?
Man had no pity on her—no, nor God—
   A nameless castaway!

But Mother Earth now hugs her to her breast,
   Defiled or undefiled;
And willows rock the weary soul to rest,
   As she, even she, her child.

THE STREET-CHILDREN'S DANCE.

NOW the earth in fields and hills
Stirs with pulses of the Spring,
Nest-embowering hedges ring
With interminable trills;
Sunlight runs a race with rain,
All the world grows young again.

Young as at the hour of birth:
From the grass the daisies rise
With the dew upon their eyes,
Sun-awakened eyes of earth;
Fields are set with cups of gold;
Can this budding world grow old?

Can the world grow old and sere,
Now when ruddy-tasselled trees
Stoop to every passing breeze,
Rustling in their silken gear;
Now when blossoms pink and white
Have their own terrestrial light?

Brooding light falls soft and warm,
Where in many a wind-rocked nest,
Curled up 'neath the she-bird's breast,
Clustering eggs are hid from harm ;
While the mellow-throated thrush
Warbles in the purpling bush.

Misty purple bathes the Spring :
Swallows flashing here and there
Float and dive on waves of air,
And make love upon the wing ;
Crocus-buds in sheaths of gold
Burst like sunbeams from the mould.

Chestnut leaflets burst their buds,
Perching tiptoe on each spray,
Springing toward the radiant day,
As the bland, pacific floods
Of the generative sun
All the teeming earth o'errun.

Can this earth run o'er with beauty,
Laugh through leaf and flower and grain,
While in close-pent court and lane,
In the air so thick and sooty,
Little ones pace to and fro,
Weighted with their parents' woe?

Woe-predestined little ones!
Putting forth their buds of life
In an atmosphere of strife,
And crime breeding ignorance;
Where the bitter surge of care
Freezes to a dull despair.

Dull despair and misery
Lie about them from their birth;
Ugly curses, uglier mirth,
Are their earliest lullaby;
Fathers have they without name,
Mothers crushed by want and shame.

Brutish, overburthened mothers,
With their hungry children cast
Half-nude to the nipping blast;
Little sisters with their brothers
Dragging in their arms all day
Children nigh as big as they.

Children mothered by the street:
Shouting, flouting, roaring after
Passers-by with gibes and laughter,
Diving between horses' feet,
In and out of drays and barrows,
Recklessly, like London sparrows.

Mudlarks of our slums and alleys,
All unconscious of the blooming
World behind those housetops looming,
Of the happy fields and valleys,
Of the miracle of Spring
With its boundless blossoming.

Blossoms of humanity !
Poor soiled blossoms in the dust !
Through the thick defiling crust
Of soul-stifling poverty,
In your features may be traced
Childhood's beauty half effaced—

Childhood, stunted in the shadow
Of the light-debarring walls :
Not for you the cuckoo calls
O'er the silver-threaded meadow ;
Not for you the lark on high
Pours his music from the sky.

Ah ! you have your music too !
And come flocking round that player
Grinding at his organ there,
Summer-eyed and swart of hue,
Rattling off his well-worn tune
On this April afternoon.

Lovely April lights of pleasure
Flit o'er want-beclouded features
Of these little outcast creatures,
As they swing with rhythmic measure,
In the courage of their rags,
Lightly o'er the slippery flags.

Little footfalls, lightly glancing
In a luxury of motion,
Supple as the waves of ocean
In your elemental dancing,
How you fly, and wheel, and spin,
For your hearts too dance within.

Dance along with mirth and laughter,
Buoyant, fearless, and elate,
Dancing in the teeth of fate,
Ignorant of your hereafter
That with all its tragic glooms
Blindly on your future looms.

Past and future, hence away!
Joy, diffused throughout the earth,
Centre in this moment's mirth
Of ecstatic holiday:
Once in all their lives' dark story,
Touch them, Fate! with April glory.

Poems of the Open Air.

THE SOWER.

THE winds had hushed at last as by command ;
    The quiet sky above,
With its grey clouds spread o'er the fallow land,
    Sat brooding like a dove.

There was no motion in the air, no sound
    Within the tree-tops stirred,
Save when some last leaf, fluttering to the ground,
    Dropped like a wounded bird :

Or when the swart rooks in a gathering crowd
    With clamorous noises wheeled,
Hovering awhile, then swooped with wranglings loud
    Down on the stubbly field.

For now the big-thewed horses, toiling slow
    In straining couples yoked,
Patiently dragged the ploughshare to and fro
    Till their wet haunches smoked.

Till the stiff acre, broken into clods,
   Bruised by the harrow's tooth,
Lay lightly shaken, with its humid sods
   Ranged into furrows smooth.

There looming lone, from rise to set of sun,
   Without or pause or speed,
Solemnly striding by the furrows dun,
   The sower sows the seed.

The sower sows the seed, which mouldering,
   Deep coffined in the earth,
Is buried now, but with the future spring
   Will quicken into birth.

Oh, poles of birth and death ! Controlling Powers
   Of human toil and need !
On this fair earth all men are surely sowers,
   Surely all life is seed !

All life is seed, dropped in Time's yawning furrow,
   Which with slow sprout and shoot,
In the revolving world's unfathomed morrow,
   Will blossom and bear fruit.

REAPERS.

SUN-TANNED men and women, toiling there
together ;
Seven I count in all, in yon field of wheat,
Where the rich ripe ears in the harvest weather
Glow an orange gold through the sweltering heat.

Busy life is still, sunk in brooding leisure :
Birds have hushed their singing in the hushed tree-
tops ;
Not a single cloud mars the flawless azure ;
Not a shadow moves o'er the moveless crops ;

In the glassy shallows, that no breath is creasing,
Chestnut-coloured cows in the rushes dank
Stand like cows of bronze, save when they flick the
teasing
Flies with switch of tail from each quivering flank.

Nature takes a rest—even her bees are sleeping,
And the silent wood seems a church that's shut ;
But these human creatures cease not from their
reaping
While the corn stands high, waiting to be cut.

THE SLEEPING BEAUTY.

THERE was intoxication in the air;
    The wind, keen blowing from across the seas,
O'er leagues of new-ploughed land and heathery leas,
Smelt of wild gorse whose gold flamed everywhere.
An undertone of song pulsed far and near,
    The soaring larks filled heaven with ecstasies,
    And, like a living clock among the trees,
The shouting cuckoo struck the time of year.

For now the Sun had found the earth once more,
    And woke the Sleeping Beauty with a kiss;
Who thrilled with light of love in every pore,
    Opened her flower-blue eyes, and looked in his.
Then all things felt life fluttering at their core—
    The world shook mystical in lambent bliss.

APPLE-BLOSSOM.

BLOSSOM of the apple trees !
    Mossy trunks all gnarled and hoary,
  Grey boughs tipped with rose-veined glory,
Clustered petals soft as fleece
Garlanding old apple trees !

How you gleam at break of day !
    When the coy sun, glancing rarely,
    Pouts and sparkles in the pearly
Pendulous dewdrops, twinkling gay
On each dancing leaf and spray.

Through your latticed boughs on high,
    Framed in rosy wreaths, one catches
    Brief kaleidoscopic snatches
Of deep lapis-lazuli
In the April-coloured sky.

When the sundown's dying brand
  Leaves your beauty to the tender
  Magic spells of moonlight splendour,
Glimmering clouds of bloom you stand,
Turning earth to fairyland.

Cease, wild winds, O, cease to blow !
  Apple-blossom, fluttering, flying,
  Palely on the green turf lying,
Vanishing like winter snow ;
Swift as joy to come and go.

A WINTER LANDSCAPE.

ALL night, all day, in dizzy, downward flight,
Fell the wild-whirling, vague, chaotic snow,
Till every landmark of the earth below,
Trees, moorlands, roads, and each familiar sight
Were blotted out by the bewildering white.
   And winds, now shrieking loud, now whimpering low,
Seemed lamentations for the world-old woe
That death must swallow life, and darkness light.

But all at once the rack was blown away,
   The snowstorm hushing ended in a sigh ;
   Then like a flame the crescent moon on high
Leaped forth among the planets ; pure as they,
Earth vied in whiteness with the Milky Way :
   Herself a star beneath the starry sky.

IN THE ST. GOTTHARDT PASS.

THE storm which shook the silence of the hills
And sleeping pinnacles of ancient snow
Went muttering off in one last thunder throe
Mixed with a moan of multitudinous rills;
Yea, even as one who has wept much, but stills
The flowing tears of some convulsive woe
When a fair light of hope begins to glow
Athwart the gloom of long remembered ills:

So does the face of this scarred mountain height
Relax its stony frown, while slow uprolled
Invidious mists are changed to veiling gold.
Wild peaks still fluctuate between dark and bright,
But when the sun laughs at them, as of old,
They kiss high heaven in all embracing light.

ROMAN ANEMONES.

THE maiden meadows softly blush
  Beneath the enamoured breeze,
And break into one purple flush
  Of frail anemones.

Violet and rose and vermeil white
  Woven of sun and showers
They seem to be embodied light
  Transfigured into flowers.

ON READING THE "RUBÁIYÁT" OF OMAR KHAYYÁM.

IN A KENTISH ROSE GARDEN.

BESIDE a Dial in the leafy close,
Where every bush was burning with the Rose,
With million roses falling flake by flake
Upon the lawn in fading summer snows:

I read the Persian Poet's rhyme of old,
Each thought a ruby in a ring of gold—
Old thoughts so young, that, after all these years,
They're writ on every rose-leaf yet unrolled.

You may not know the secret tongue aright
The Sunbeams on their rosy tablets write;
Only a poet may perchance translate
Those ruby-tinted hieroglyphs of light.

THE MOAT.

AROUND this lichened home of hoary peace,
  Invulnerable in its glassy moat,
A breath of ghostly summers seems to float
And murmur 'mid the immemorial trees.
The tender slopes, where cattle browse at ease,
  Swell softly, like a pigeon's emerald throat;
  And, self-oblivious, Time forgets to note
The flight of velvet-footed centuries.

The golden sunshine, netted in the close,
  Sleeps indolently by the Yew's slow shade;
  Still as some relic an old Master made
The jewelled peacock's rich enamel glows;
And on yon mossy wall that youthful rose
  Blooms like a rose which never means to fade.

ON A TORSO OF CUPID.

PEACH trees and Judas trees,
   Poppies and roses,
Purple anemones
   In garden closes !
Lost in the limpid sky,
Shrills a gay lark on high ;
Lost in the covert's hush,
Gurgles a wooing thrush.

Look, where the ivy weaves,
   Closely embracing,
Tendrils of clinging leaves
   Round him enlacing,
With Nature's sacredness
Clothing the nakedness,
Clothing the marble of
This poor, dismembered love.

ON A TORSO OF CUPID.

Gone are the hands whose skill
    Aimed the light arrow,
Strong once to cure or kill,
    Pierce to the marrow ;
Gone are the lips whose kiss
Held hives of honeyed bliss ;
Gone too the little feet,
Overfond, overfleet.

O helpless god of old,
    Maimed mid the tender
Blossoming white and gold
    Of April splendour !
Shall we not make thy grave
Where the long grasses wave ;
Hide thee, O headless god,
Deep in the daisied sod ?

Here thou mayst rest at last
    After life's fever ;
After love's fret is past
    Rest thee for ever.
Nay, broken God of Love,
Still must thou bide above
While, left for woe or weal,
Thou hast a heart to feel.

THE MIRROR OF DIANA.

SHE floats into the quiet skies,
   Where, in the circle of the hills,
   Her immemorial mirror fills
With light, as of a Virgin's eyes
When, love a-tremble in their blue,
They glow twin violets dipped in dew.

Mild as a metaphor of Sleep,
   Immaculately maiden-white,
   The Queen Moon of ancestral night
Beholds her image in the deep:
As if a-gaze she beams above
Like Nemi's magic glass of love.

White rose, white lily of the vale,
   Perfume the even breath of night;
   In many a burst of sweet delight
The love throb of the nightingale
Swells through lush flowering woods and fills
The circle of the listening hills.

White rose, white lily of the skies,
  The Moon-flower blossoms in the lake;
  The nightingale for her fair sake
With hopeless love's impassioned cries
Seems fain to sing till song must kill
Himself with one tumultuous trill.

And all the songs and all the scents,
  The light of glowworms and the fires
  Of fire-flies in the cypress spires;
And all the wild wind instruments
Of pine and ilex as the breeze
Sweeps out their mystic harmonies;

All are but Messengers of May
  To that white orb of maiden fire
  Who fills the moth with mad desire
To die enamoured in her ray,
And turns each dewdrop in the grass
Into a fairy looking-glass.

O Beauty, far and far above
  The night moth and the nightingale!
  Far, far above life's narrow pale,
O Unattainable! O Love!
Even as the nightingale we cry
For some Ideal set on high.

Haunting the deep reflective mind,
   You may surprise its perfect Sphere
   Glassed like the Moon within her mere,
Who at a puff of alien wind
Melts in innumerable rings,
Elusive in the flux of things.

Love in Exile and Other Love Poems

LOVE IN EXILE.

I.

SHE stood against the Orient sun,
   Her face inscrutable for light;
A myriad larks in unison
Sang o'er her, soaring out of sight.

A myriad flowers around her feet
Burst flame-like from the yielding sod,
Till all the wandering airs were sweet
With incense mounting up to God.

A mighty rainbow shook, inclined
Towards her, from the Occident,
Girdling the cloud-wrack which enshrined
Half the light-bearing firmament.

Lit showers flashed golden o'er the hills,
And trees flung silver to the breeze,
And, scattering diamonds, fleet-foot rills
Fled laughingly across the leas.

Yea, Love, the skylarks laud but thee,
And writ in flowers thine awful name;
Spring is thy shade, dread Ecstasy,
And life a brand which feeds thy flame.

II.

Winding all my life about thee,
  Let me lay my lips on thine ;
What is all the world without thee,
  Mine—oh mine !

Let me press my heart out on thee,
  Grape of life's most fiery vine,
Spilling sacramental on thee
  Love's red wine.

Let thy strong eyes yearning o'er me
  Draw me with their force divine ;
All my soul has gone before me
  Clasping thine.

Irresistibly I follow,
  As wherever we may run
Runs our shadow, as the swallow
  Seeks the sun.

Yea, I tremble, swoon, surrender
All my spirit to thy sway,
As a star is drowned in splendour
Of the day.

III.

I charge you, O winds of the West, O winds with the
 wings of the dove,
That ye blow o'er the brows of my Love, breathing
 low that I sicken for love.

I charge you, O dews of the Dawn, O tears of the
 star of the morn,
That ye fall at the feet of my love with the sound of
 one weeping forlorn.

I charge you, O birds of the Air, O birds flying home
 to your nest,
That ye sing in his ears of the joy that for ever has
 fled from my breast.

I charge you, O flowers of the Earth, O frailest of
 things, and most fair,
That ye droop in his path as the life in me shrivels
 consumed by despair.

O Moon, when he lifts up his face, when he seeth the
  waning of thee,
A memory of her who lies wan on the limits of life
  let it be.

Many tears cannot quench, nor my sighs extinguish,
  the flames of love's fire,
Which lifteth my heart like a wave, and smites it, and
  breaks its desire.

I rise like one in a dream when I see the red sun
  flaring low,
That drags me back shuddering from sleep each
  morning to life with its woe.

I go like one in a dream, unbidden my feet know the
  way
To that garden where love stood in blossom with the
  red and white hawthorn of May.

The song of the throstle is hushed, and the fountain
  is dry to its core,
The moon cometh up as of old; she seeks, but she
  finds him no more.

The pale-faced, pitiful moon shines down on the grass
    where I weep,
My face to the earth, and my breast in an anguish
    ne'er soothed into sleep.

The moon returns, and the spring, birds warble, trees
    burst into leaf,
But Love once gone, goes for ever, and all that
    endures is the grief.

IV.

Thou walkest with me as the spirit-light
Of the hushed moon, high o'er a snowy hill,
Walks with the houseless traveller all the night,
    When trees are tongueless and when mute the rill.
Moon of my soul, O phantasm of delight,
    Thou walkest with me still.

The vestal flame of quenchless memory burns
    In my soul's sanctuary. Yea, still for thee
My bitter heart hath yearned, as moonward yearns
    Each separate wave-pulse of the clamorous sea:
My Moon of love, to whom for ever turns
    The life that aches through me.

V.

I think of thee in watches of the night,
    I feel thee near;
Like mystic lamps consumed with too much light
    Thine eyes burn clear.

The barriers that divide us in the day
    And hide from view,
Like idle cobwebs now are brushed away
    Between us two.

I probe the deep recesses of thy mind
    Without control,
And in its inmost labyrinth I find
    My own lost soul.

No longer like an exile on the earth
    I wildly roam,
I was thy double from the hour of birth
    And thou my home.

VI.

I was again beside thee in a dream:
    Earth was so beautiful, the moon was shining;
The muffled voice of many a cataract stream
    Came like a love-song, as, with arms entwining,
Our hearts were mixed in unison supreme.

The wind lay spell-bound in each pillared pine,
    The tasselled larches had no sound or motion,
As my whole life was sinking into thine—
    Sinking into a deep, unfathomed ocean
Of infinite love—uncircumscribed, divine.

Night held her breath, it seemed, with all her stars;
    Eternal eyes that watched in mute compassion
Our little lives o'erleap their mortal bars,
    Fused in the fulness of immortal passion,
A passion as immortal as the stars.

There was no longer any thee or me;
    No sense of self, no wish or incompleteness
The moment, rounded to Eternity,
    Annihilated time's destructive fleetness;
For all but love itself had ceased to be.

VII.

Our souls have touched each other,
   Two fountains from one jet ;
Like children of one mother
   Our leaping thoughts have met.

We were as far asunder
   As green isles in the sea :
And now we ask in wonder
   How that could ever be.

I dare not call thee lover
   Nor any earthly name,
Though love's full cup flows over
   As water quick with flame.

When two strong minds have mated
   As only spirits may,
The world shines new created
   In a diviner day.

Yea, though hard fate may sever
My fleeting self from thine,
Thy thought will live for ever
And ever grow in mine.

VIII.

I am athirst, but not for wine ;
The drink I long for is divine,
Poured only from your eyes in mine.

I hunger, but the bread I want,
Of which my blood and brain are scant,
Is your sweet speech, for which I pant.

I am a-cold, and lagging lame,
Life creeps along my languid frame ;
Your love would fan it into flame.

Heaven's in that little word—your love !
It makes my heart coo like a dove,
My tears fall as I think thereof.

IX.

I would I were the glow-worm, thou the flower,
   That I might fill thy cup with glimmering light
I would I were the bird, and thou the bower,
   To sing thee songs throughout the summer night.

I would I were a pine tree deeply rooted,
   And thou the lofty, cloud-beleaguered rock,
Still, while the blasts of heaven around us hooted,
   To cleave to thee and weather every shock.

I would I were the rill, and thou the river;
   So might I, leaping from some headlong steep,
With all my waters lost in thine for ever,
   Be hurried onwards to the unfathomed deep.

I would—what would I not? O foolish dreaming,
   My words are but as leaves by autumn shed,
That, in the faded moonlight idly gleaming,
   Drop on the grave where all our love lies dead.

LOVE IN EXILE.

X.

The woods shake in an ague-fit,
   The mad wind rocks the pine,
From sea to sea the white gulls flit
   Into the roaring brine.

The moon as if in panic grief
   Darts through the clouds on high,
Blown like a wild autumnal leaf
   Across the wilder sky.

The gusty rain is driving fast,
   And through the rain we hear,
Above the equinoctial blast,
   The thunder of the Weir.

The voices of the wind and rain
   Wail echoing through my heart—
That love is ever dogged by pain
   And fondest souls must part.

You made heart's summer, O my friend,
   But now we bid adieu,
There will be winter without end
   And tears for ever new.

XI.

Dost thou remember ever, for my sake,
When we two rowed upon the rock-bound lake?
How the wind-fretted waters blew their spray
About our brows like blossom-falls of May
    One memorable day?

Dost thou remember the glad mouth that cried—
"Were it not sweet to die now side by side,
To lie together tangled in the deep
Close as the heart-beat to the heart—so keep
    The everlasting sleep?"

Dost thou remember? Ah, such death as this
Had set the seal upon my heart's young bliss!
But, wrenched asunder, severed and apart,
Life knew a deadlier death: the blighting smart
    Which only kills the heart.

XII.

Like some wild sleeper who alone at night
Walks with unseeing eyes along a height,
   With death below and only stars above :
I, in broad daylight, walk as if in sleep,
Along the edges of life's perilous steep,
   The lost somnambulist of love.

I, in broad day, go walking in a dream,
Led on in safety by the starry gleam
   Of thy blue eyes that hold my heart in thrall ;
Let no one wake me rudely, lest one day,
Startled to find how far I've gone astray,
   I dash my life out in my fall.

XIII.

O moon, large golden summer moon,
   Hanging between the linden trees,
   Which in the intermittent breeze
Beat with the rhythmic pulse of June !

O night-air, scented through and through
   With honey-coloured flower of lime,
   Sweet now as in that other time
When all my heart was sweet as you !

The sorcery of this breathing bloom
   Works like enchantment in my brain,
   Till, shuddering back to life again,
My dead self rises from its tomb.

And, lovely with the love of yore,
   Its white ghost haunts the moon-white ways;
   But, when it meets me face to face,
Flies trembling to the grave once more.

XIV.

I planted a rose tree in my garden,
  In early days when the year was young;
I thought it would bear me roses, roses,
  While nights were dewy and days were long.

It bore but once, and a white rose only—
  A lovely rose with petals of light;
Like the moon in heaven, supreme and lonely;
  And the lightning struck it one summer night.

XV.

Why will you haunt me unawares,
   And walk into my sleep,
Pacing its shadowy thoroughfares,
Where long-dried perfume scents the airs,
   While ghosts of sorrow creep,
Where on Hope's ruined altar-stairs,
   With ineffectual beams,
The Moon of Memory coldly glares
   Upon the land of dreams?

My yearning eyes were fain to look
   Upon your hidden face;
Their love, alas! you could not brook,
But in your own you mutely took
   My hand, and for a space
You wrung it till I throbbed and shook,
   And woke with wildest moan
And wet face channelled like a brook
   With your tears or my own.

XVI.

When you wake from troubled slumbers
   With a dream-bewildered brain,
And old leaves which no man numbers
   Chattering tap against the pane ;
And the midnight wind is wailing
Till your very life seems quailing
    As the long gusts shudder and sigh :
    Know you not that homeless cry
    Is my love's, which cannot die,
    Wailing through Eternity ?

When beside the glowing embers,
   Sitting in the twilight lone,
Drop on drop you hear November's
   Melancholy monotone,
As the heavy rain comes sweeping,
With a sound of weeping, weeping,
    Till your blood is chilled with fears ;
    Know you not those falling tears,
    Flowing fast through years on years,
    For my sobs within your ears ?

When with dolorous moan the billows
  Surge around where, far and wide,
Leagues on leagues of sea-worn hollows
  Throb with thunders of the tide,
And the weary waves in breaking
Fill you, thrill you, as with aching
  Memories of our love of yore,
  Where you pace the sounding shore,
  Hear you not, through roll and roar,
  Soul call soul for evermore?

XVII.

In a lonesome burial-place
Crouched a mourner white of face ;
　Wild her eyes—unheeding
Circling pomp of night and day—
Ever crying, "Well away,
　Love lies a-bleeding ! "

And her sighs were like a knell,
And her tears for ever fell,
　With their warm rain feeding
That purpureal flower, alas !
Trailing prostrate in the grass,
　Love lies a-bleeding.

Through the yews' black-tufted gloom
Crimson light fell on the tomb,
　Funeral shadows breeding :
In the sky the sun's light shed
Dyed the earth one awful red—
　Love lies a-bleeding.

Came grey mists, and blanching cloud
Bore one universal shroud;
  Came the bowed moon leading,
From the infinite afar
Star that rumoured unto star—
  Love lies a-bleeding.

XVIII.

Deep in a yew-sequestered grove
I sat and wept my heart away;
A child came by at close of day
With eyes as sweet as new-born love.

He came from sun-bleached meadows where
High on the hedge the topmost rose
Curtsies to every wind that blows,
A wanton of the summer air.

The sunset aureoled his brow,
Kindling the roses in his hand,
And by my side I saw him stand
To offer me his rose-red bough:

Take back thy gift—I sighed forlorn,
And showed where like the yew's red seed,
My blood had trickled, bead on bead,
From wounds made by his cruel thorn.

He smiled and said :—Nay, take my Rose;
You know, when all is said and done,
There's not a joy beneath the sun
Worth lovers' joys but lovers' woes.

XIX.

On life's long round by chance I found
  A dell impearled with dew ;
Where hyacinths, gushing from the ground,
  Lent to the earth heaven's native hue
  Of holy blue.

I sought that plot of azure light
  Once more in gloomy hours ;
But snow had fallen overnight
  And wrapped in mortuary white
  My fairy ring of flowers.

XX.

Ah, yesterday was dark and drear,
    My heart was deadly sore ;
Without thy love it seemed, my Dear,
    That I could live no more.

And yet I laugh and sing to-day ;
    Care or care not for me,
Thou canst not take the love away
    With which I worship thee.

And if to-morrow, Dear, I live,
    My heart I shall not break :
For still I hold it that to give
    Is sweeter than to take.

XXI.

I took your face into my dreams,
   It floated round me like a light;
Your beauty's consecrating beams
   Lay mirrored in my heart all night.
As in a lonely mountain mere,
   Unvisited of any streams,
Supremely bright and still and clear,
   The solitary moonlight gleams,
Your face was shining in my dreams.

XXII.

We met as strangers on life's lonely way,
    And yet it seemed we knew each other well;
There was no end to what thou hadst to say,
    Or to the thousand things I found to tell.
My heart, long silent, at thy voice that day
    Chimed in my breast like to a silver bell.

How much we spoke, and yet still left untold
    Some secret half revealed within our eyes:
Didst thou not love me once in ages old?
    Had I not called thee with importunate cries,
And, like a child left sobbing in the cold,
    Listened to catch from far thy fond replies?

We met as strangers, and as such we part;
    Yet all my life seems leaving me with thine;
Ah, to be clasped once only heart to heart,
    If only once to feel that thou wert mine!
These lips are locked, and yet I know thou art
    That all in all for which my soul did pine.

XXIII.

You make the sunshine of my heart
   And its tempestuous shower;
Sometimes the thought of you is like
   A lilac bush in flower,
Yea, honey-sweet as hives in May.
And then the pang of it will strike
My bosom with a fiery smart,
As though love's deeply planted dart
   Drained all its life away.

My thoughts hum round you, Dear, like bees
   About a bank of thyme,
Or round the yellow blossoms of
   The heavy-scented lime.
Ah, sweeter you than honeydew,
   Yet dark the ways of love,
For it has robbed my soul of peace,
And marred my life and turned heart's-ease
   Into funereal rue.

XXIV.

Ah, if you knew how soon and late
   My eyes long for a sight of you,
Sometimes in passing by my gate
   You'd linger until fall of dew,
     If you but knew!

Ah, if you knew how sick and sore
   My life flags for the want of you,
Straightway you'd enter at the door
   And clasp my hand between your two,
     If you but knew!

Ah, if you knew how lost and lone
   I watch and weep and wait for you,
You'd press my heart close to your own
   Till love had healed me through and through,
     If you but knew!

XXV.

Your looks have touched my soul with bright
    Ineffable emotion ;
As moonbeams on a stormy night
Illume with transitory light
A seagull on her lonely flight
    Across the lonely ocean.

Fluttering from out the gloom and roar,
    On fitful wing she flies,
Moon-white above the moon-washed shore ;
Then, drowned in darkness as before,
She's lost, as I when lit no more
    By your beloved eyes.

XXVI.

What magic is there in thy mien,
   What sorcery in thy smile,
Which charms away all cark and care,
Which turns the foul days into fair,
   And for a little while
Changes this disenchanted scene
From the sere leaf into the green,
   Transmuting with love's golden wand
   This beggared life to fairyland?

My heart goes forth to thee, oh friend,
   As some poor pilgrim to a shrine,
A pilgrim who has come from far
To seek his spirit's folding star,
   And sees the taper shine;
The goal to which his wanderings tend,
Where want and weariness shall end,
   And kneels ecstatically blest
   Because his heart hath entered rest.

L'ENVOI.

THOU art the goal for which my spirit longs ;
    As dove on dove,
Bound for one home, I send thee all my songs
    With all my love.

Thou art the haven with fair harbour lights ;
    Safe locked in thee,
My heart would anchor after stormful nights
    Alone at sea.

Thou art the rest of which my life is fain,
    The perfect peace ;
Absorbed in thee the world, with all its pain
    And toil, would cease.

Thou art the heaven to which my soul would go
    O dearest eyes,
Lost in your light you would turn hell below
    To Paradise.

Thou all in all for which my heart-blood yearns !
   Yea, near or far—
Where the unfathomed ether throbs and burns
   With star on star,

Or where, enkindled by the fires of June,
   The fresh earth glows,
Blushing beneath the mystical white moon
   Through rose on rose—

Thee, thee I see, thee feel in all live things,
   Beloved one ;
In the first bird which tremulously sings
   Ere peep of sun ;

In the last nestling orphaned in the hedge,
   Rocked to and fro,
When dying summer shudders in the sedge,
   And swallows go ;

When roaring snows rush down the mountain-pass,
   March floods with rills,
Or April lightens through the living grass
   In daffodils ;

L'ENVOI.

When poppied cornfields simmer in the heat
    With tare and thistle,
And, like winged clouds above the mellow wheat,
    The starlings whistle;

When stained with sunset the wide moorlands glare
    In the wild weather,
And clouds with flaming craters smoke and flare
    Red o'er red heather;

When the bent moon, on frostbound midnights waking,
    Leans to the snow
Like some world-mother, whose deep heart is breaking
    O'er human woe.

As the round sun rolls red into the ocean,
    Till all the sea
Glows fluid gold, even so life's mazy motion
    Is dyed with thee:

For as the wave-like years subside and roll,
    O heart's desire,
Thy soul glows interfused within my soul,
    A quenchless fire.

Yea, thee I feel, all storms of life above,
   Near though afar ;
O thou my glorious morning star of love,
   And evening star.

THE SONGS OF SUMMER.

THE songs of summer are over and past !
  The swallow's forsaken the dripping eaves ;
  Ruined and black 'mid the sodden leaves
The nests are rudely swung in the blast :
  And ever the wind like a soul in pain
  Knocks and knocks at the window-pane.

The songs of summer are over and past !
  Woe's me for a music sweeter than theirs—
  The quick, light bound of a step on the stairs,
The greeting of lovers too sweet to last :
  And ever the wind like a soul in pain
  Knocks and knocks at the window-pane.

ON AND ON.

BY long leagues of wood and meadow
   On and on we drive apace ;
In the dreamy light and shadow
   Veiling earth's autumnal face.

Rosy clouds are drifting o'er us,
   Rooks rise parleying from their tryst,
And the road lies far before us,
   Fading into amethyst.

On and on, through leagues of heather,
   Deeps of scarlet beaded lane,
Like a pheasant's golden feather
   Golden leaves around us rain.

On and on, where woodlands hoary,
   In October's lavish fire,
Flame up with unearthly glory,
   Beauteous summer's funeral pyre.

On and on, where casements blinking
  Lighten into transient gules,
As the dying day in sinking
  Splashes all the wayside pools.

On and on ; the land grows dimmer,
  And our road recedes afar ;
While on either hand there glimmer
  Setting sun and rising star.

Would I knew what thoughts steal o'er you,
  As the long road lengthens yet :
Ah, like hope it winds before you,
  And behind me like regret.

CROSS-ROADS.

THE rain beat in our faces,
   And shrill the wild airs grew;
The long-maned clouds in races
   Coursed o'er heaven's windy blue.

The tortured trees were lashing
   Each other in their wrath,
Their wet leaves wildly dashing
   Across the forest path.

We did not heed the sweeping
   Of storm-bewildered rain;
Our cheeks were wet with weeping,
   Our hearts were wrung with pain.

For where the cross-roads sever,
   Parting to East and West,
We bade good-bye for ever
   To what we each loved best.

THE FOREST POOL.

LOST amid gloom and solitude,
A pool lies hidden in the wood,
A pool the autumn rain has made
Where flowers with their fair shadows played.

Bare as a beggar's board the trees
Stand in the water to their knees;
The birds are mute, but far away
I hear a bloodhound's sullen bay.

Blue-eyed forget-me-nots that shook,
Kissed by a little laughing brook,
Kissed too by you with lips so red,
Float in the water drowned and dead.

And dead and drowned, 'mid leaves that rot,
Our angel-eyed Forget-me-not,
The love of unforgotten years,
Floats corpse-like in a pool of tears.

ONCE WE PLAYED.

ONCE we played at love together—
Played it smartly, if you please;
Lightly, as a wind-blown feather,
Did we stake a heart apiece.

Oh, it was delicious fooling!
In the hottest of the game,
Without thought of future cooling,
All too quickly burned Life's flame.

In this give-and-take of glances,
Kisses sweet as honey dews,
When we played with equal chances,
Did you win, or did I lose?

Was your heart then hurt to bleeding,
In the ardour of the throw?
Was it then I lost, unheeding,
Lost my heart so long ago?

Who shall say? The game is over.
Of us two who loved in fun,
One lies low beneath the clover,
One lives lonely in the sun.

ONLY A SMILE.

NO butterfly whose frugal fare
    Is breath of heliotrope and clove,
And other trifles light as air,
    Could live on less than doth my love.

That childlike smile that comes and goes
    About your gracious lips and eyes,
Hath all the sweetness of the rose,
    Which feeds the freckled butterflies.

I feed my love on smiles, and yet
    Sometimes I ask, with tears of woe,
How had it been if we had met,
    If you had met me long ago,

Before the fast, defacing years
    Had made all ill that once was well?
Ah, then your smiling breeds such tears
    As Tantalus may weep in hell.

SOMETIMES I WONDER.

SOMETIMES I wonder if you guess
The deep impassioned tenderness
  Which overflows my heart ;
The love I never dare confess ;
Yet hard, yea, harder to repress
  Than tears too fain to start.

Sometimes I ponder, O my sweet,
The things I'll tell you when we meet ;
  But straightway at your sight
My heart's blood oozes to my feet
Like thawing waters in the heat,
  Confused with too much light.

I hardly know, when you are near,
If it is love, or joy, or fear
  Which fills my languid frame ;
Enveloped in your atmosphere,
My dark self seems to disappear,
  A moth entombed in flame.

MANY WILL LOVE YOU.

M ANY will love you; you were made for love;
   For the soft plumage of the unruffled dove
  Is not so soft as your caressing eyes.
You will love many; for the winds that veer
Are not more prone to shift their compass, dear,
  Than your quick fancy flies.

Many may love you; but I may not, no;
Even though your smile sets all my life aglow,
  And at your fairness all my senses ache.
You will love many; but not me, my dear,
Who have no gift to give you but a tear
  Sweet for your sweetness' sake.

AFFINITIES.

I.

I WILL take your thoughts to my heart;
   I will keep and garner them there
Locked in a casket apart.
   Far above rubies or rare
Pearls from the prodigal deep,
   Which men stake their lives on to find,
And women their beauty to keep,
   I will treasure the pearls of your mind.

How long has it taken the earth
   To crystallize gems in a mine?
How long was the sea giving birth
   To her pearls, washed in bitterest brine?
What sorrows, what struggles, what fierce
   Endeavour of lives in the past,
Hearts tempered by fire and tears,
   To fashion your manhood at last!

II.

Take me to thy heart, and let me
  Rest my head a little while;
Rest my heart from griefs that fret me
  In the mercy of thy smile.

In a twilight pause of feeling,
  Time to say a moment's grace,
Put thy hands, whose touch is healing,
  Put them gently on my face.

Found too late in Life's wild welter,
  All I ask, for weal and woe,
Friend, a moment's friendly shelter,
  And thy blessing ere I go.

III.

Full many loves and friendships dear
  Have blossomed brightly in my path;
  And some were like the primrose rathe,
And withered with the vernal year.

And some were like the joyous rose,
  Most prodigal with scent and hue,
  That glows while yet the sky is blue,
And falls with every wind that blows—

Mere guests and annuals of the heart;
But you are that perennial bay,
Greenest when greener leaves decay,
Whom only death shall bid depart.

Songs and Sonnets

SONG.

OH haste while roses bloom below,
    Oh haste while pale and bright above
The sun and moon alternate glow,
    To pluck the rose of love.

Yea, give the morning to the lark,
The nightingale its glimmering grove,
Give moonlight to the hungry dark,
    But to man's heart give love!

Then haste while still the roses blow,
And pale and bright in heaven above
The sun and moon alternate glow,
    Pluck, pluck the rose of love.

PASTICHE.

LOVE, oh, Love's a dainty sweeting,
Wooing now, and now retreating;
Brightest joy and blackest care,
Swift as light, and light as air.

Would you seize and fix and capture
All his evanescent rapture?
Bind him fast with golden curls,
Fetter with a chair of pearls?

Would you catch him in a net,
Like a white moth prankt with jet?
Clutch him, and his bloomy wing
Turns a dead, discoloured thing!

Pluck him like a rosebud red,
And he leaves a thorn instead;
Let him go without a care
And he follows unaware.

Love, oh, Love's a dainty sweeting,
Wooing now, and now retreating;
Lightly come, and lightly gone,
Lost when most securely won!

A FANTASY.

I WAS an Arab,
  I loved my horse;
Swift as an arrow
  He swept the course.

Sweet as a lamb
  He came to hand;
He was the flower
  Of all the land.

Through lonely nights
  I rode afar;
God lit His lights—
  Star upon star.

God's in the desert;
  His breath the air:
Beautiful desert,
  Boundless and bare.

Free as the wild wind,
  Light as a foal;
Ah, there is room there
  To stretch one's soul.

Far reached my thought,
  Scant were my needs;
A few bananas
  And lotus seeds.

Sparkling as water
  Cool in the shade,
Ibrahim's daughter,
  Beautiful maid,

Out of thy Kulleh,
  Fairest and first,
Give me to drink,
  Quencher of thirst.

I am athirst, girl;
  Parched with desire,
Love in my bosom
  Burns as a fire.

Green thy oasis,
  Waving with Palms;
Oh, be no niggard,
  Maid, with thy alms.

Kiss me with kisses,
  Buds of thy mouth,
Sweeter than Cassia
  Fresh from the South.

Bind me with tresses,
  Clasp with a curl;
And in caresses
  Stifle me, girl.

I was an Arab
  Ages ago!
Hence this home sickness
  And all my woe.

ON A VIOLA D'AMORE.

CARVED WITH A CUPID'S HEAD, AND PLAYED ON FOR THE FIRST TIME AFTER MORE THAN A CENTURY.

WHAT fairy music clear and light,
   Responsive to your fingers,
Swells rippling on the summer night,
   And amorously lingers
Upon the sense, as long ago
In days of rouge and rococo!

A century of silence lay
   On strings that had not spoken
Since powdered lords to ladies gay
   Gave, for a lover's token,
Fans glowing fresh from Watteau's art,
Well worth a marchioness's heart.

Your dormant music tranced and bound
  Was like the Sleeping Beauty
Prince Charming in the forest found,
  And kissed in loyal duty :
And when she woke her eyes, blue fire
Turned the dumb forest to a lyre.

Thus Amor with the bandaged eyes
  Fit symbol of hushed numbers,
Most musically wakes and sighs
  After an age of slumbers :
Beneath your magic bow's control
The Viol has regained her soul.

SOUL-DRIFT.

I LET my soul drift with the thistledown
    Afloat upon the honeymooning breeze ;
My thoughts about the swelling buds are blown,
    Blown with the golden dust of flowering trees.

On fleeting gusts of desultory song,
    I let my soul drift out into the Spring ;
The Psyche flies and palpitates among
    The palpitating creatures on the wing.

Go, happy Soul ! run fluid in the wave,
    Vibrate in light, escape thy natal curse ;
Go forth no longer as my body-slave,
    But as the heir of all the Universe.

LASSITUDE.

I LAID me down beside the sea,
Endless in blue monotony;
The clouds were anchored in the sky,
Sometimes a sail went idling by.

Upon the shingles on the beach
Grey linen was spread out to bleach,
And gently with a gentle swell
The languid ripples rose and fell.

A fisher-boy, in level line,
Cast stone by stone into the brine:
Methought I too might do as he,
And cast my sorrows on the sea.

The old, old sorrows in a heap
Dropped heavily into the deep;
But with its sorrow on that day
My heart itself was cast away.

REST.

WE are so tired, my heart and I.
 Of all things here beneath the sky
One only thing would please us best—
Endless, unfathomable rest.

We are so tired; we ask no more
Than just to slip out by Life's door;
And leave behind the noisy rout
And everlasting turn about.

Once it seemed well to run on too
With her importunate, fevered crew,
And snatch amid the frantic strife
Some morsel from the board of life.

But we are tired. At Life's crude hands
We ask no gift she understands;
But kneel to him she hates to crave
The absolution of the grave.

Sonnets

SLEEP.

LOVE-CRADLING Night, lit by the lucent moon,
Most pitiful and mother-hearted Night!
Blest armistice in life's tumultuous fight,
Resolving discords to a spheral tune!
When tired with heat and strenuous toil of noon,
With ceaseless conflict betwixt might and right,
With ebb and flow of sorrow and delight,
Our panting hearts beneath their burdens swoon,

To thee, O star-eyed comforter, we creep,
Earth's ill-used step-children to thee make moan,
As hiding in thy dark skirts' ample sweep;
—Poor debtors whose brief life is not their own;
For dunned by Death, to whom we owe its loan,
Give us, O Night, the interest paid in sleep.

DEAD LOVE.

MOTHER of the unfortunate, mystic form,
Who calm, immutable, like oldest fate,
Sittest, where through the sombre swinging gate
Moans immemorial life's encircling storm.
My heart, sore stricken by grief's leaden arm,
Lags like a weary pilgrim knocking late,
And sigheth—toward thee staggering with its weight—
Behold Love conquered by thy son, the worm!

He stung him 'mid the roses' purple bloom,
The Rose of roses, yea, a thing so sweet,
Haply to stay blind Change's flying feet,
And stir with pity the unpitying tomb.
Here, take him, cold, cold, heavy and void of breath!
Nor me refuse, O Mother almighty, death.

DESPAIR.

THY wings swoop darkening round my soul,
   Despair !
And on my brain thy shadow seems to brood
And hem me round with stifling solitude,
With chasms of vacuous gloom which are thy lair.
No light of human joy, no song or prayer,
Breaks ever on this chaos, all imbrued
With heart's-blood trickling from the multitude
Of sweet hopes slain, or agonising there.

Lo, wilt thou yield thyself to grief, and roll
Vanquished from thy high seat, imperial brain ;
And, abdicating turbulent life's control,
Be dragged a captive bound in sorrow's chain?
Nay ! though my heart is breaking with its pain,
No pain on earth has power to crush my soul.

CLEAVE THOU THE WAVES.

CLEAVE thou the waves that weltering to and fro
Surge multitudinous. The eternal Powers
Of sun, moon, stars, the air, the hurrying hours,
The winged winds, the still dissolving show
Of clouds in calm or storm, for ever flow
Above thee ; while the abysmal sea devours
The untold dead insatiate, where it lowers
O'er glooms unfathomed, limitless, below.

No longer on the golden-fretted sands,
Where many a shallow tide abortive chafes,
Mayst thou delay ; life onward sweeping blends
With far-off heaven : the dauntless one who braves
The perilous flood with calm unswerving hands,
The elements sustain : cleave thou the waves.

THE DEAD.

THE dead abide with us! Though stark and cold
Earth seems to grip them, they are with us still:
They have forged our chains of being for good or ill;
And their invisible hands these hands yet hold.
Our perishable bodies are the mould
In which their strong imperishable will—
Mortality's deep yearning to fulfil—
Hath grown incorporate through dim time untold.

Vibrations infinite of life in death,
As a star's travelling light survives its star!
So may we hold our lives, that when we are
The fate of those who then will draw this breath,
They shall not drag us to their judgment bar,
And curse the heritage which we bequeath.

HOPE.

ALL treasures of the earth and opulent seas,
Metals and odorous woods and cunning gold,
Fowls of the air and furry beasts untold,
Vineyards and harvest fields and fruitful trees
Nature gave unto Man; and last her keys
Vouched passage to her sacred ways of old
Whence knowledge should be wrung, nay power to mould
Out of the rough, his occult destinies.

But tired of these he craved a wider scope :
Then fair as Pallas from the brain of Jove
From his deep wish there sprang, full-armed, to cope
With all life's ills, even very death in love,
The only thing man never wearies of—
His own creation—visionary Hope.

TIME'S SHADOW.

THY life, O Man, in this brief moment lies :
   Time's narrow bridge whereon we darkling
     stand,
With an infinitude on either hand
Receding luminously from our eyes.
Lo, there thy Past's forsaken Paradise
   Subsideth like some visionary strand,
   While glimmering faint, the Future's promised land,
Illusive from the abyss, seems fain to rise.

This hour alone Hope's broken pledges mar,
   And Joy now gleams before, now in our rear,
Like mirage mocking in some waste afar,
   Dissolving into air as we draw near.
   Beyond our steps the path is sunny-clear,
The shadow lying only where we are.

SUFFERING.

OH ye, all ye, who suffer here below,
    Schooled in the baffling mystery of pain,
Who on life's anvil bear the fateful strain,
Wrung as forged iron, hammered blow on blow.
Take counsel with your grief, in that you know,
That he who suffers suffers not in vain,
Nay, that it shall be for the whole world's gain,
And wisdom prove the priceless price of woe.

Thus in some new-found land where no man's feet
Have trod a path, bold voyagers astray
May fall foredone by torturing thirst and heat:
But, from the impotent body of defeat,
The winners spring who carve a conquering way,
Measured by milestones of their perished clay.

ΑΝΑΓΚΗ.

L IKE a great rock which looming o'er the deep
       Casts his eternal shadow on the strands,
And veiled in cloud inexorably stands,
While vaulting round his adamantine steep
Embattled breakers clamorously leap,
Sun-garlanded and hope-uplifted bands,
But soon with waters shattered in the sands
Slowly recoiling back to ocean creep:

So sternly dost thou tower above us, Fate!
For still our eager hearts exultant beat,
Borne in the hurrying tide of life elate,
And dashing break against thy marble feet.
But would Hope's rainbow aureole round us fleet,
Without these hurtling shocks of man's estate?

TO MEMORY.

OH in this dearth and winter of the soul,
    When even Hope, still wont to soar and sing,
Droopeth, a starveling bird whose downy wing
Stiffens ere dead through the dank drift it fall—
Yea, ere Hope perish utterly, I call
On thee, fond Memory, that thou haste and bring
One leaf, one blossom from that far-off spring
When love's auroral light lay over all.

Bring but one pansy : haply so the thrill
Of poignant yearning for those glad dead years
May, like the gusty south, breathe o'er the chill
Of frozen grief, dissolving it in tears,
Till numb Hope, stirred by that warm dropping rain,
Will deem, perchance, Love's springtide come again.

·THE AFTER-GLOW.

IT is a solemn evening, golden-clear—
The Alpine summits flame with rose-lit snow,
And headlands purpling on wide seas below,
And clouds and woods and arid rocks appear
Dissolving in the sun's own atmosphere
   And vast circumference of light, whose slow
   Transfiguration—glow and after-glow—
Turns twilight earth to a more luminous sphere.

O heart, I ask, seeing that the orb of day
Has sunk below, yet left to sky and sea
   His glory's spiritual after-shine:
I ask if Love, whose sun hath set for thee,
May not touch grief with his memorial ray,
   And lend to loss itself a joy divine?

MANCHESTER BY NIGHT.

O 'ER this huge town, rife with intestine wars,
Whence as from monstrous sacrificial shrines
Pillars of smoke climb heavenward, Night inclines
Black brows majestical with glimmering stars.
Her dewy silence soothes life's angry jars :
And like a mother's wan white face, who pines
Above her children's turbulent ways, so shines
The moon athwart the narrow cloudy bars.

Now toiling multitudes that hustling crush
Each other in a fateful strife for breath,
And, hounded on by diverse hungers, rush
Across the prostrate ones that groan beneath,
Are swathed within the universal hush,
As life exchanges semblances with death.

THE RED SUNSETS, 1883.

THE twilight heavens are flushed with gathering light,
And o'er wet roofs and huddling streets below
Hang with a strange Apocalyptic glow
On the black fringes of the wintry night.
Such bursts of glory may have rapt the sight
    Of him to whom on Patmos long ago
    The visionary angel came to show
That heavenly city built of chrysolite.

And lo, three factory hands begrimed with soot,
    Aflame with the red splendour, marvelling stand,
And gaze with lifted faces awed and mute.
    Starved of earth's beauty by Man's grudging hand,
O toilers, robbed of labour's golden fruit,
    Ye, too, may feast in Nature's fairyland.

THE SÂKIYEH.

"How long shall Man be Nature's fool?" Man
cries;
"Be like those great, gaunt oxen, drilled and bound,
Inexorably driven round and round
To turn the water-wheel with bandaged eyes?
And as they trudge beneath Egyptian skies,
Watering the wrinkled desert's beggared ground,
The hoarse Sâkiyeh's lamentable sound
Fills all the land as with a people's sighs?"

Poor Brutes! who in unconsciousness sublime,
Replenishing the ever-empty jars,
Endow the waste with palms and harvest gold:
And men, who move in rhythm with moving stars,
Should shrink to give the borrowed lives they
hold:
Bound blindfold to the groaning wheel of Time.

MOURNING WOMEN.

ALL veiled in black, with faces hid from sight,
Crouching together in the jolting cart,
What forms are these that pass alone, apart
In abject apathy to life's delight?
The motley crowd, fantastically bright,
   Shifts gorgeous through each dazzling street and mart;
   Only these sisters of the suffering heart
Strike discord in this symphony of light.

Most wretched women! whom your prophet dooms
   To take love's penalties without its prize!
Yes; you shall bear the unborn in your wombs,
   And water dusty death with streaming eyes,
And, wailing, beat your breasts among the tombs;
   But souls ye have none fit for Paradise.

THE AGNOSTIC.

NOT in the hour of peril, thronged with foes,
   Panting to set their heel upon my head,
Or when alone from many wounds I bled
Unflinching beneath Fortune's random blows;
Not when my shuddering hands were doomed to close
   The unshrinking eyelids of the stony dead;—
   Not then I missed my God, not then—but said:
"Let me not burden God with all man's woes!"

But when resurgent from the womb of night
   Spring's Oriflamme of flowers waves from the sod;
   When peak on flashing Alpine peak is trod
By sunbeams on their missionary flight;
When heaven-kissed Earth laughs, garmented in light;—
That is the hour in which I miss my God.

HEART'S-EASE.

AS opiates to the sick on wakeful nights,
    As light to flowers, as flowers in poor men's
        rooms,
    As to the fisher when the tempest glooms
The cheerful twinkling of his village lights;
As emerald isles to flagging swallow flights,
    As roses garlanding with tendrilled blooms
    The unweeded hillocks of forgotten tombs,
As singing birds on cypress-shadowed heights,

Thou art to me—a comfort past compare—
    For thy joy-kindling presence, sweet as May
    Sets all my nerves to music, makes away
With sorrow and the numbing frost of care,
    Until the influence of thine eyes' bright sway
Has made life's glass go up from foul to fair.

UNTIMELY LOVE.

PEACE, throbbing heart, nor let us shed one tear
   O'er this late love's unseasonable glow ;
  Sweet as a violet blooming in the snow,
The posthumous offspring of the widowed year,
That smells of March when all the world is sere,
   And, while around the hurtling sea-winds blow—
   Which twist the oak and lay the pine tree low—
Stands childlike in the storm and has no fear.

Poor helpless blossom orphaned of the sun,
   How could it thus brave winter's rude estate ?
   Oh love, more helpless love, why bloom so late,
Now that the flower-time of the year is done?
Since thy dear course must end when scarce begun,
   Nipped by the cold touch of untoward fate.

CHRISTMAS EVE.

ALONE—with one fair star for company,
The loveliest star among the hosts of night,
While the grey tide ebbs with the ebbing light—
I pace along the darkening wintry sea.
Now round the yule-log and the glittering tree
Twinkling with festive tapers, eyes as bright
Sparkle with Christmas joys and young delight,
As each one gathers to his family.

But I—a waif on earth where'er I roam—
Uprooted with life's bleeding hopes and fears
From that one heart that was my heart's sole home,
Feel the old pang fierce through the severing years,
And as I think upon the years to come
That fair star trembles through my falling tears.

THE EVENING OF THE YEAR.

WAN mists enwrap the still-born day;
    The harebell withers on the heath;
And all the moorland seems to breathe
The hectic beauty of decay.
Within the open grave of May
Dishevelled trees drop wreath on wreath;
Wind-wrung and ravelled underneath
Waste leaves choke up the woodland way.

The grief of many partings near
Wails like an echo in the wind:
The days of love lie far behind,
The days of loss lie shuddering near.
Life's morning-glory who shall bind?
It is the evening of the year.

NEW YEAR'S EVE.

ANOTHER full-orbed year hath waned to-day,
And set in the irrevocable past,
And headlong whirled along Time's winged blast
My fluttering rose of youth is borne away :
Ah rose once crimson with the blood of May,
A honeyed haunt where bees would break their fast,
I watch thy scattering petals flee aghast,
And all the flickering rose-lights turning grey.

Poor fool of life ! plagued ever with thy vain
Regrets and futile longings ! were the years
Not cups o'erbrimming still with gall and tears ?
Let go thy puny personal joy and pain !
If youth with all its brief hope disappears,
To deathless hope we must be born again.

NIRVANA.

DIVEST thyself, O Soul, of vain desire!
    Bid hope farewell, dismiss all coward fears;
Take leave of empty laughter, emptier tears,
And quench, for ever quench, the wasting fire
Wherein this heart, as in a funeral pyre,
    Aye burns, yet is consumed not. Years on years
    Moaning with memories in thy maddened ears—
Let at thy word, like refluent waves, retire.

Enter thy soul's vast realm as Sovereign Lord,
And, like that angel with the flaming sword,
    Wave off life's clinging hands. Then chains will fall
From the poor slave of self's hard tyranny—
And Thou, a ripple rounded by the sea,
    In rapture lost be lapped within the All.

www.ingramcontent.com/pod-product-compliance
Lightning Source LLC
Chambersburg PA
CBHW030316170426
43202CB00009B/1021